EDGE BOOKS

WORLD RECORD BREAKERS

THE WORLD'S FASTEST MOTORCYCLES

BY ASHLEY P. WATSON NORRIS

Leslie Kendall, Curator
Petersen Automotive Museum,
Los Angeles, California, USA

Raintree is an imprint of Capstone Global Library Limited, a company incorporated in England and Wales having its registered office at 264 Banbury Road, Oxford, OX2 7DY – Registered company number: 6695582

www.raintree.co.uk
myorders@raintree.co.uk

Edited by Mandy Robbins
Designed by Sarah Bennett
Picture research by Morgan Walters
Production by Laura Manthe
Printed and bound in China.

ISBN 978-1-4747-1160-9
21 20 19 18 17
10 9 8 7 6 5 4 3 2 1

British Library Cataloguing in Publication Data
A full catalogue record for this book is available from the British Library.

Acknowledgements
We would like to thank the following for permission to reproduce photographs: David Whealon, 11; Dreamstime: Typhoonski, 15; Getty Images: Heritage Images, 5; Glow Images: Deposit Photos, 16-17; Mike Akatiff, 27, 28; Newscom: REBECCA COOK/ REUTERS, 22; Phil Hawkins, 20; Shutterstock: betto rodrigues, 18, Bykofoto, 19, Eky Studio, design element, FotoYakov, design element, DEmax, design element, Mikael Damkier, 7, Morphart Creation, top 9, Rainer Herhaus, cover, Seraphim Art, design element, Wiktoria Pawlak, design element; Tara Bogart, 10; Wikimedia: cole24_, 24, The Motorcycle Illustrated, bottom 9, Wendyhoney, 12

CONTENTS

SPEED IS KING!. 4

CHAPTER 1
THE FIRST V-8 MOTORCYCLE. 8

CHAPTER 2
THE FASTEST DIRT BIKE 10

CHAPTER 3
THE FASTEST DIESEL MOTORCYCLE. 12

CHAPTER 4
A SPEED LEADER IN PRODUCTION MOTORCYCLES 14

CHAPTER 5
FAST AND EXPENSIVE. 16

CHAPTER 6
FASTEST PRODUCTION TRACK MOTORCYCLE. 18

CHAPTER 7
THE FASTEST ELECTRIC MOTORCYCLE. 20

CHAPTER 8
TOO FAST TO RIDE 22

CHAPTER 9
STREAMLINED SPEED 24

CHAPTER 10
THE FASTEST OF THE FAST 26

GLOSSARY 30
FIND OUT MORE. 31
COMPREHENSION QUESTIONS. 31
INDEX 32

SPEED IS KING!

Humans discovered the need for motorized speed in the late 1800s and early 1900s. This was an exciting time of invention, especially for vehicles. Animals were no longer needed to haul people from place to place. Motorcycles were invented around 1885. At that time they looked like bicycles with engines. But it didn't take long for engineers to begin pushing the limits of motorcycle speed and power.

The first motorcycle racers competed against automobiles. These races were held in Europe in the late 1890s. They were typically road races from town to town. In the United States, the first all-motorcycle race was held in Los Angeles, California, in 1901.

In the 1910s and 1920s, motorcycle races in the United States were held on wooden racetracks. These racing motorcycles were built for speed, not safety. They reached speeds of up to 161 kilometres (100 miles) per hour and didn't have brakes. Wrecks were common and often deadly.

Motorcycle racer J.A. Watson-Bourne poses on a Brough motorcycle with company founder George Brough in the 1920s.

ENGINES

Over the years, motorcycle racing has grown and changed. Strict safety rules keep riders and fans safe. There are divisions for different engine sizes, rider ages and skill levels. One thing has remained the same, though – the desire to go fast.

Motorcycles use different types of engines. The engines can be compared in a couple of different measures. Cubic centimetres (cc) is a unit of volume showing how much air or liquid can be found in a cube that is 1 centimetre on every side. For vehicles, cubic centimetres measure how much volume is in the **cylinder**. The bigger the number, the more powerful the engine. Horsepower usually describes a car engine's power. It is sometimes also used when referring to an uncommonly powerful motorcycle. The more horsepower a vehicle has, the more power it has to push itself forward.

cylinder hollow area inside an engine in which fuel burns to create power

Motocross engines range in power from 50-cc to 450-cc.

CHAPTER 1

THE FIRST V-8 MOTORCYCLE

The world's first V-8 motorcycle was the Curtiss Custom V-8. A V-8 engine is one that has eight cylinders set in a "V" shape. American Glenn Curtiss custom-built his V-8 engine for a **dirigible**. He later put the engine on a custom-made 2.4-metre (8-foot) long motorcycle frame.

The power from Curtiss' 40-horsepower engine went to the rear wheel. To stop, a rider shifted his weight onto a device on the back tyre. At top speed the motorcycle took 1.6 kilometres (1 mile) to stop.

Curtiss wanted to find out how fast his motorcycle would go before giving it to the customer. On 24 January 1907, he set a speed record, blasting the V-8 motorcycle down the beach at 219.4 kilometres (136.3 miles) per hour. The Curtiss V-8 motorcycle was the fastest vehicle in the world in 1907. No car, boat, motorcycle or train had ever gone that fast.

dirigible aircraft that is powered by a motor and filled with a gas that makes it rise

dirigible

Glenn Curtiss poses on the Curtiss V-8 in 1907.

CHAPTER 2

THE FASTEST DIRT BIKE

The Wolbrink Race KX500 is the world's fastest dirt bike. As a dirt bike, it can go off-road on rough **terrain**. After the race team modified it for land speed racing, Kevin Kilkenny set its fastest record of 211.5 kilometres (131.418 miles) per hour in 2008.

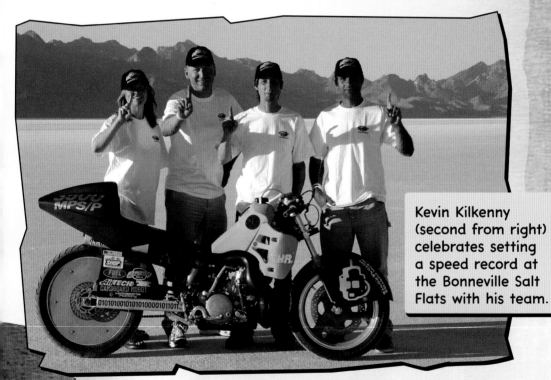

Kevin Kilkenny (second from right) celebrates setting a speed record at the Bonneville Salt Flats with his team.

RACING LOCATIONS

Races for the fastest motorcycle speeds are held in many places. The most famous is the Bonneville Salt Flats in Utah, USA. It is 119 square kilometres (46 square miles) of hard, flat, salt-covered land that is perfect for straight-line racing.

The Wolbrink Race team started with a **stock** Kawasaki KX500 dirt bike. They bought it for £3,500 and spent another £3,500 to fine-tune the performance of its engine. The stock KX500 is very tall. The rider has to stand on a bench and wear a heavy boot to kick-start the bike. In preparation for Kilkenny riding the bike, the team lowered the suspension. Smaller wheels, different gearing and sleek bodywork were added to make the bike as fast as possible. At top speed, this KX500 can go only 8 kilometres (5 miles) before it runs out of petrol.

terrain surface of the land

stock vehicle that has all of the parts that were installed at the factory

CHAPTER 3

THE FASTEST DIESEL MOTORCYCLE

The Crucible Die-Moto rocketed down the Bonneville Salt Flats at just over 209 kilometres (130 miles) per hour in 2007. This feat made it the fastest diesel motorcycle in the world.

The Crucible Die-Moto runs on biodiesel instead of petrol. The switch to biodiesel reduced the bike's pollution by 78 per cent. Biodiesel is an environmentally friendly alternative to petrol.

Crucible founder Michael Sturtz takes the Die-Moto for a test ride.

A group of artists, engineers and motorcycle fans built the Die-Moto. They wanted to prove that motorcycles can be fast and environmentally friendly.

The Die-Moto is 3 metres (9.8 feet) long and weighs 499 kilograms (1,100 pounds). This odd-looking motorcycle is pieced together from many different vehicles. It has a 163-horsepower BMW diesel car engine and two Honda car **radiators**. It also has BMW motorcycle **forks**, steering components and wheels. The frame and all the other parts are custom-made.

The Die-Moto requires a lot of skill and concentration to ride. Engineers could not convert all the car pieces to work like a normal motorcycle should. The clutch for shifting gears uses a right foot pedal like a car instead of a lever on the right handlebar like a motorcycle. The rider leans forward on his chest to operate the bike and extends his right leg backwards to shift gears. When the driver shifts, the bike can lean. At high speeds, this can be dangerous.

radiator part of the vehicle through which the fluid flows so that it can be cooled

fork part of a motorcycle that connects the front wheel and axle to the bike frame

FACT

Riders wear a lot of gear to protect their bodies. Gear includes helmets, special boots, padded jackets and trousers.

CHAPTER 4

A SPEED LEADER IN PRODUCTION MOTORCYCLES

The Suzuki Hayabusa is among the fastest **production** motorcycles in the world. Stock models reach 299 kilometres (186 miles) per hour.

Hayabusa means "peregrine falcon" in Japanese. Suzuki channelled the power of this mighty bird in building its motorcycle of the same name. The bike has a 1,340-cc engine. Despite its amazing performance capabilities, the Hayabusa is accessible to the public. It costs about £10,600 and is mass-produced.

A highly customized Hayabusa set a record of 502 kilometres (311.945 miles) per hour in 2011 at Loring Air Force Base in Maine, USA. This bike had a turbocharger and custom **aerodynamic fairings**. Its speed made it the fastest open-cockpit motorcycle ever timed.

production describes a vehicle manufactured for mass-market sale

aerodynamic ability of something to move easily and quickly through the air

fairing outer covering of a motorcycle that helps the bike cut through the air

In 2000 motorcycle makers agreed to limit speed in production motorcycles. Most of today's mass-produced, road-worthy bikes are limited to a top speed of 299 kilometres (186 miles) per hour.

TIMING MOTORCYCLE SPEED

A precise process is used to time motorcycle speed during a land speed race. In land speed racing one motorcycle travels in a straight line to set a speed record. Electronic equipment sends a beam of light across the racetrack to a receiver. When a motorcycle breaks the light beam, its speed can be calculated.

The Hayabusa is a street-legal motorcycle.

CHAPTER 5

FAST AND EXPENSIVE

The MTT Y2K **Turbine** Superbike holds two Guinness World Records. It is the most powerful production motorcycle built since 2000. It is also the most expensive production motorcycle. This £130,000 bike has been clocked at speeds of around 402 kilometres (250 miles) per hour. It can go from 0 to 60 miles (96.5 kilometres) per hour in 1.4 seconds.

The MTT Y2K Turbine has a Rolls-Royce petrol turbine engine that is used in helicopters. The engine produces more than 420 horsepower. The heat coming out of the back of the engine can melt the bumper of a car following too close behind it.

turbine engine powered by steam or petrol; the steam or petrol moves through the blades of a fan-like device and makes the device turn

FACT

Marine Turbine Technologies produces only four or five Y2Ks per year.

CHAPTER 6
FASTEST PRODUCTION TRACK MOTORCYCLE

New to the market, the 2015 Kawasaki Ninja H2 may reach speeds of 451 kilometres (280 miles) per hour. It has a 998-cc engine with a supercharger. The bike is priced at £21,200. Only a limited number will be sold each year.

Wind tunnel testing was used to create the aerodynamic body design of the Ninja H2. Wings on the front create **downforce**. They keep the bike from lifting off the ground at high speeds.

This motorcycle is meant to be driven on the racetrack only and comes with racing slick tyres. It does not have rearview mirrors, indicators or other parts needed for street-legal bikes. Buyers of a Ninja H2 have to sign a form agreeing not to drive it on public roads.

2015 Kawasaki Ninja H2

The Ninja H2 is loud. Noise is measured in **decibels**, and the Ninja H2 measures 120 decibels. That's as loud as a rock concert or ambulance siren. It can cause permanent hearing loss.

Racers lean into a curve during a 2015 Moto Grand Prix race in Spain.

MOTORCYCLE RACING

Many different types of motorcycle races exist, including motocross, endurance, road races and ice races. Different types of bikes are designed for each type of racing. Moto Grand Prix is an 18-race series with multiple **superbikes**, such as the Ninja H2, racing around a track at the same time.

downforce force of passing air pressing down on a moving vehicle

decibel unit for measuring the volume of sounds

superbike high-performance motorcycle with a large engine, usually between 800 and 1,200-cc

CHAPTER 7

THE FASTEST ELECTRIC MOTORCYCLE

The KillaJoule is the world's fastest electric motorcycle. It also holds the record for the world's fastest sidecar motorcycle. Its official speed record is 386 kilometres (240 miles) per hour. Its top speed so far is 434.5 kilometres (270 miles) per hour.

Electric motorcycles and cars are becoming more common every day. They are important because they are better for the environment. A standard combustion engine burns petrol. An electric vehicle runs on batteries that are rechargeable. They are recharged by special high-voltage electric cords. It usually takes a few hours to recharge a vehicle.

The KillaJoule blasts down Utah's Salt Flats in 2012.

The KillaJoule is a completely enclosed motorcycle called a streamliner. It is shaped like a teardrop or bullet. It is designed to move through the air as quickly as possible. The fairing covers the entire motorcycle, including the wheels and rider. The KillaJoule runs on 224 battery cells. Together these cells weigh 136 kilograms (300 pounds). The KillaJoule's batteries cost £10,600.

The KillaJoule is 5.8 metres (19 feet) long and weighs 698.5 kilograms (1,540 pounds). It took a year to build. The battery cells produce power equal to 400 horsepower.

After every run, the batteries take two hours to recharge. During a land speed race, the team switches out the batteries for fresh ones for the second timed run.

The owner, designer and pilot of this bullet was Eva Hakansson. The KillaJoule's world record of 434.5 kilometres (270 miles) per hour makes Hakansson the fastest woman on a motorcycle!

FACT

Riders of streamlined vehicles, such as the KillaJoule, are also called pilots or drivers. "Pilots" is used because these vehicles go fast like a jet. "Drivers" is used because people sit in the motorcycle instead of riding on it. All three terms are correct.

CHAPTER 8

TOO FAST TO RIDE

The builders of the Dodge Tomahawk describe it as a sculpture that can be ridden. This bike is not street-legal. It weighs 680 kilograms (1,500 pounds). That's two to three times what most **cruiser**-style motorcycles weigh. The Tomahawk has two front tyres and two back tyres. They help the motorcycle remain stable and get enough traction to speed up. It has headlights located between the front wheels.

Dodge introduced the Tomahawk at a US auto show in 2003.

cruiser style of motorcycle where the rider is slightly reclined

This beast of a motorcycle has a Dodge Viper car engine. The engine can propel the bike to speeds estimated at 483 to 563 kilometres (300 to 350 miles) per hour.

The rider sits on top of the bike, unprotected from the wind. Its top speed has not been tested because the machine would be unsafe for the rider. At around 322 kilometres (200 miles) per hour the wind would actually lift the rider up out of the seat.

The V-10 Viper engine pumps out an astounding 500 horsepower. It can push the Tomahawk from 0 to 60 miles (97 kilometres) per hour in 2.5 seconds!

STRAIGHT OUT OF A FILM

Two Dodge employees asked their bosses for permission to build a motorcycle with a Viper V-10 engine. Their vision was inspired by the four-wheeled motorcycle shown in the 1982 film *Tron*. From concept to completion it took their team eight months to build the first Dodge Tomahawk.

FACT

The Dodge Tomahawk costs £389,000. Only nine have ever been built.

CHAPTER 9

STREAMLINED SPEED

The Bub 7 has set several world records. In 2006 it set a land speed record at just over 563 kilometres (350 miles) per hour. That record was broken in 2008. But in 2009 the Bub 7 reclaimed the world land speed record at 591 kilometres (367 miles) per hour. Its top recorded speed during the race was 599 kilometres (372 miles) per hour.

The Bub 7 looks more like a missile than a motorcycle.

The Bub 7 streamliner was designed for one purpose – to break the land speed record. It pumps out 500 horsepower through its turbocharged 3,000-cc engine. The pilot, Chris Carr, covered 1.6 kilometres (1 mile) in less than 10 seconds! Designed and built from scratch, it is an engineering marvel. The steering controls are the same ones found in an F-4 Phantom fighter jet. The clutch is from an Indy race car.

The Bub 7 runs on methanol, a fuel used in some race cars. Methanol lights on fire at a higher temperature than petrol. A methanol fire can also be extinguished with water. That is important for pilot and team safety.

RECORD CHASERS

A lot of time, effort and money go into the design and building of a high-speed motorcycle meant to break world speed records. The owners, team members and pilots chase the dream of holding a land speed record. A land speed record cannot be owned. It is only borrowed until the next speed-demon comes along to challenge the title.

CHAPTER 10

THE FASTEST OF THE FAST

The Ack Attack is the fastest motorcycle in the world. It set the record of 605 kilometres (376 miles) per hour at the Bonneville Salt Flats in 2010. Its official top speed is 634 kilometres (394 miles) per hour. Unofficially it can pass 644 kilometres (400 miles) per hour.

The Ack Attack motorcycle is a streamliner more than 5.8 metres (19 feet) long. It has two 1,300-cc Suzuki Hayabusa engines with turbochargers and 16 kilograms (35 pounds) of boost. These features help the engine reach 1,000 horsepower.

The Ack Attack uses 118-octane petrol. It guzzles 15.5 litres (4.1 gallons) of petrol during an 18-kilometre (11-mile) run. Its two racing tyres are designed for speeds of more than 805 kilometres (500 miles) per hour. The Ack Attack has two chains that combine the power of the two engines.

To stop the Ack Attack, the pilot squeezes the right hand brake lever to release a parachute. Even with the parachute it takes 8 kilometres (5 miles) to fully stop the Ack Attack.

The Ack Attack looked like a giant blue bullet blasting down the Bonneville Salt Flats.

FACT

The Ack Attack is faster than a Ferrari, Lamborghini or Porsche sports car.

Rocky Robinson has been the pilot for all three of the Ack Attack's record-setting runs. In 2006 he set a world record on Ack Attack at just under 552 kilometres (343 miles) per hour. In 2008 he beat his previous world record by going 580.8 kilometres (360.913 miles) per hour. Robinson's 2010 run holds the world record at 605 kilometres (376 miles) per hour. He is one of the four people in the world qualified to drive a streamline motorcycle. Every time Robinson drives, he always carries a different good luck charm in his pocket.

With high speed comes danger, and the Ack Attack has been in three serious crashes. In the biggest crash it was going faster than 483 kilometres (300 miles) per hour. It rolled 16 times, but Robinson walked away without serious injuries.

Pilot safety is a priority. The pilot is strapped into the bike with a nine-point safety harness. Arm and leg restraints are locked into the safety harness. During a crash, the harness and restraints keep the pilot's entire body safely inside the motorcycle. The bike has two fire prevention systems. The pilot wears a **fire-retardant** racing suit, gloves, boots and head sock. The helmet has a fire-retardant lining.

The Ack Attack may currently hold the title of the world's fastest motorcycle, but it won't forever. If one thing is certain, it's that humans love nothing more than pushing limits, and the limits of speed are no exception. Only time will tell how fast the motorcycles of the future will go.

Rocky Robinson (centre, wearing cap) poses with his team next to the Ack Attack.

fire-retardant chemical that prevents a fire from spreading

GLOSSARY

aerodynamic ability of something to move easily and quickly through the air

cruiser style of motorcycle where the rider is sitting upright or slightly reclined

custom specially done or made

cylinder hollow area inside an engine in which fuel burns to create power

decibel unit for measuring the volume of sounds

dirigible aircraft that is powered by a motor and filled with a gas that makes it rise

downforce force of passing air pressing down on a moving vehicle

fairing outer covering of a motorcycle that helps the bike cut through air

fire-retardant chemical that prevents a fire from spreading

fork part of a motorcycle that connects the front wheel and axle to the bike frame

production describes a vehicle manufactured for mass-market sale

radiator part of the vehicle through which the fluid flows so that it can be cooled

restraint something that holds someone back

stock vehicle that has all of the parts that were installed at the factory

superbike high-performance motorcycle with a large engine, usually between 800 and 1,200-cc

terrain surface of the land

turbine engine powered by steam or petrol; the steam or petrol moves through the blades of a fan-like device and makes it turn

FIND OUT MORE

BOOKS

First Book of Bikes and Motorbikes (Bloomsbury Transport Collection), Isabel Thomas (A&C Black Children's & Educational, 2014)

MotoGP Rider: Marc Macquez vs Valentino Rossi (The Inside Track), Paul Mason (Franklin Watts, 2016)

Motorbikes, Lisa Gillespie (Usborne, 2011)

WEBSITES

Haynes International Motor Museum
www.haynesmotormuseum.com

KillaJoule
killacycleracing.com/about-us/killajoule/

UK National Motor Museum
www.nationalmotormuseum.org.uk/

COMPREHENSION QUESTIONS

1. Why do you think that the world's fastest motorcycles are not usually sold to the public?

2. Loring Air Force Base in Maine, USA, and the Bonneville Salt Flats in Utah, USA, are both places where speed records have been set. What type of land features do you think are ideal when it comes to chasing land speed records?

INDEX

Ack Attack 26–29

biodiesel 12
Bonneville Salt Flats 10, 12, 26
Bub 7 24–25

Carr, Chris 25
Crucible Die-Moto 12–13
Curtiss Custom V-8 8
Curtiss, Glenn 8

Dodge Tomahawk 22–23

electric vehicles 20–21

Hakansson, Eva 21

Kawasaki Ninja H2 18, 19
Kilkenny, Kevin 10, 11
KillaJoule 20–21

methanol 25
motorcycle history 4
motorcycle racing 4, 6, 10, 15,
    18, 19, 21, 24, 26
MTT Y2K Turbine Superbike
    16, 17

petrol 11, 12, 20, 25, 26

records 8, 10, 11, 12, 14, 15, 20,
    21, 24, 25, 26, 28
  Guinness World Records 16
  land speed records 15, 24, 25
Robinson, Rocky 28

safety 4, 6, 25, 29
streamliners 21, 25, 26, 28
superchargers 18
Suzuki Hayabusa 14, 26

turbochargers 14, 25, 26

Wolbrink, Mark 11
Wolbrink Race KX500 10–11